Ticker-tape

Ticker-tape
Rishi Dastidar

ISBN: 978-1911027171

First published March 2017 by:

Nine Arches Press
PO Box 6269
Rugby
CV21 9NL
United Kingdom

www.ninearchespress.com

Printed in Britain by:
The Russell Press Ltd.

Nine Arches Press is supported using public funding by the National Lottery through Arts Council England.

Supported using public funding by
**ARTS COUNCIL
ENGLAND**

Ticker-tape

Rishi Dastidar

Nine
Arches
Press

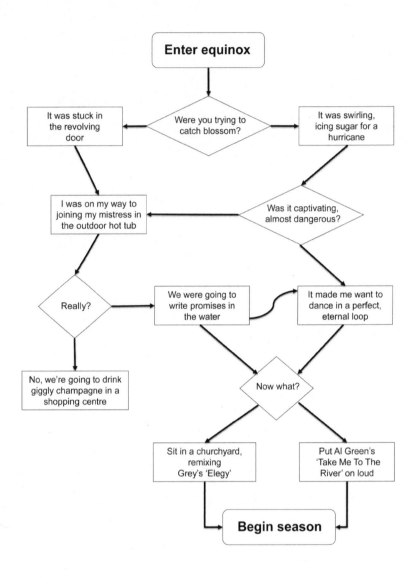

Contents

Parades go by /
So many beautiful parades go by /
Leave me behind

– The Magnetic Fields

The summers of Camus' youth

In Algiers, you don't talk about 'going swimming'
but 'knocking off for a swim'.

I won't insist.

People swim in the harbour
and then go rest on the buoys.

When you pass a buoy
where a pretty girl is sitting,

you shout to your friends,
"I tell you it's a seagull".

These are healthy pleasures.
They certainly seem ideal to the young men.

The Girl Boy Black White Urban Desert Digital Blues Rhinestone Drone Desire

This is the first | the first in a series of agreeable gestures |
The delta is an open microphone | eleven strings tie us to you |

We will make you slaves | to dopamine fixes and ludic dreaming |
We don't pick our heels up when we leave | We will make you
    like us more |

We are picking a fight | with the self-deluding structures of life |
We are salved | We will blast you by the hymns of our youth |

Thank you for being 15 minutes late for breakfast |
Renaming this stream 'Notes on Yearning' |

The more we say | the more we betray ourselves |
Who can afford | such luxuries anymore? |

The full-throated maximalists | modern greats generalists |
Managing for the age of managed decline |

We're soundtracking a vision as big as the world |
Yes Cupid untying the zone of a link girl |

Why won't the algorithms protect us from the past? |
Oh hai infinite loop of memory |

See the past comebackatcha | and shiver |
We give you the eternal ability to remember the thing you least
    want to |

We have collapsed | into the permanent now |
Into gravity's grave | the projection of this project |

We'll teach you to be street | sweet, replicants, rhinestone crust |
on paprika skin | Dreamt of your avatar last night | left tears on
    your hair |

We are the girl boy you never slept with | that you want to forget |
We pout and rattle to infinity | Can we objectify you yeah |

This imperative mood is infectious | This imperative mood infects us |
This is a manifesto for us | This is a manifesto for the cosmic us |

Trunk shavasana

(a/k/a the bliss of incantation makes it good to be alive)

And the concomitant sky came down to meet you
And history's rubber vines came down to meet you
And the dreams of muscle clouds came down to meet you
And the long-hoodied ponies came down to meet you
And the gleam of kudos and chrome came down to meet you
And the sweet ride of a continent's youth came down to meet you
And the quadriga's thundering embrace came down to hold you
And the rabona's *blaugrana* arc came down to meet you
And the collated astronauts came down to meet you
And the cities of bespoke newsprint folded down to meet you
And the sharp-suited white nights came down to meet you
And the infinite heart's sighs came down to meet you
And the angels on workfare placements came down to meet you
And this timorous Shiva, with hands unsheathed, will come to you

Deconstructing an attempted date with Miss Pacific Standard Time

1. You are a refugee of over-achievement from the once, and coming-again-now continent.

2. She is leaning alluringly out of a moving tramcar, taking a selfie.

3. You flutter your smarter timepieces at Miss PST.

4. It is unclear whether the tramcar cares. Its headlights are blinking.

5. She is biding. You might be good for Rebel Purdah Evening.

6. She has a big idea. She calls it 'a restoration of local time zones, with church steeples as meridians.'

7. …but what of disappointment and unreliability?

8. *"Post* as is to truth as *pre* as is to apocalypse."

9. "There will always be a divine surplus for kids."

10. She absolutely, categorically, without reservation, refutes the idea we're in The Overblown Age.

11. Gold and peace, iron and war. Gold and peace, iron and war.

12. "I am scratched, damaged, tectonically faulted too."

13. Everyone is always Saint Sebastian in their own story.

14. "If you say so, darl."

A shark comes to dinner

Well it's not a shark as such, more the nebbish simile
Woody Allen used in *Annie Hall*, the one about how
Marshall McLuhan has to keep moving forward to
massage the message. Anyway the dorsal fin is frantically

    stirring the pot fretting that the lobsters, squash and carrots
    haven't been chopped finely enough according to the proto-
    hipster aesthetic because, would you credit it,
    him with the teeth is afraid to bleed.

'Potluck *Kinfolk* style' she'd said, and he'd flapped a happy yes
not knowing what two out of those three words meant, but hey!
what did it matter? He'd seen enough *Masterchefs* to know you
just had to do a journey, a chocolate fondant and some Alpine
microherbs, then your life changed. Imagine the shock

    when he discovered that an induction hob could be as dangerous
    as a pedestal, and she wasn't going to undo her apron for any
    old Jawsy-Come-Lately brandishing Elizabeth David's come hither
    Mediterranean words. 'Calm' she commanded, as she swept him

onto the table, and bade him wait upon her homemade pastrami.
He looked over and tried to drool attractively. You've never seen
a mammal wish so fervently to tell Linnaeus to stuff himself,
become a slice of rye bread, gherkins, English mustard on the side.

Contour

In every map is a kind of trance,
a whisper that insists geography
is destiny, no matter what you say.
Remember the bridges of Königsberg,
the whisper continues. That was an unsolvable
problem, and so is your desire to keep
moving, to lose yourself in whatever
new topography you can conjure
with the spin of a compass –
as if it's a roulette wheel,
rather than a divining rod
that keeps reminding you
he who changes the sky above him
without changing his soul changes nothing.

From Stavanger

I have been up for 23 hours now,
teetering on the edge of
missing home / missing her,

and it's all I can do to resist
the entreaties for one more
slice of Norwegian salmon,

sound the retreat to the empty seat
in the one-desk terminal as I wait
for the propellers of my ride

to cut through the lassitude of the clouds
and get me rolling down the coast,
over triumphant Hanseatic business deals.

But there is no such thing
as a straight line above this earth,
so we prowl above Amsterdam,

a commuter eagle at weary bay, until
the crook finger of the jet bridge beckons
and I run slide glide perspire

curse cry drag squeak careen
to the beacon-jacketed help, who
with a smile of relaxed molasses says,

"Sir, there's another connection in 45 minutes.
Why not let Schiphol be your home for now?
We have a beautiful sunset here too."

Doom loop

In this *pilot episode*

    for a micro-crisis satisfaction is satiation;
    of course I am bored of having too many options,
    too many voices from the social cacophony to reconcile,
    too much time to think about too little,
    bored of striking angular poses I can't hold,

            how the hope and change thing never works out,
          unmoored by her mismatching bra, nails and wedges

                       commercials

    how writers inflict their versions of *Moby-Dick* on me,
               like I don't have mine to live;

    only yes people and satraps prosper here;
    the more in this loop I thrash, the more I use
    screamers in my blipverts to the outside world – 'I am fine!!!'
    always is the opposite; there is a German word for all this,
    I am sure   but fucked if Google Translate knows it.

Roll credits

"THE PACIFIC OCEAN IS BECOMING CAFFEINATED"

The story goes on to allege that the sea is
the inheritor of mass-produced secrets and prancing
with the ecstatic release of doing something well.

You see ships in the harbour, made of biodegradable
dixie cups, orange peel sails and lemongrass rigging.
Saxifrage semaphore warns of understudied contaminants,

then entreats: 'World questions King's answers?' If only.
The world answers a King's questions, as it always
has done. He always wins communiqué chess;

with the softest binding, his promises wrapped in silk
evasions, billed to an invisible ink transcription service.
"Stuff the relevant guns with green tissue paper?

Oh how we tried, and look where that got us."
You shove a reusable hemp shopping bag
over your head, go besting for your hope.

Matchstick Empire

*"So what do you say, now give me a
nice cup of hot, good, real English tea."*
 – Wilhelm II on entering exile, 1918

He had followed the laws of expansion
in the manner of his tippling grandmother,
but alas ended up so unworthy a sovereign

that he could only wear blue serge suits,
loden capes and a hunting hat –
though he couldn't shoot any more,

nor ride – just walk, feed the ducks
and cut down trees, twenty thousand
by his seventieth birthday. He joked

this harvest was the only *Gedankensplitter**
his people would listen to now.
The logs went to the faithful poor,

the only retinue left; or became matchsticks
given to the curious, with no mention made
of the fire passing between empty hands.

*collection of aphorisms

21

22 March, Working in an Office on Berners Street

It is four days and half an average lifetime
after a simile happened to Richard Brautigan

elsewhere, half an ocean away.
Nothing has happened to me

except that the sun has come out
for the first time in my life

the way the light comes on when you open
a fridge, and two slices of last night's pizza

are waiting to be breakfasted upon.
In 38 years time, the Met Office and the news app

won't be able to tell you what happened, but trust me,
it's as true as the expression on your face right now.

Licking stamps

Let me guess, painter boy. You'll depict me
as your Emma Hamilton in that Romney portrait,
all cheesecloth and Circe,
before moving onto some nonsense
about how I'm an antebellum babe
and that you have a battleplan for courting,
to neuter my Gatling gun tongue.
And then you'll have me say something
like, 'I want to be ravaged like Dresden
in 1945', when clearly I want to be
ravaged like Northumbria in 865.
But still, really, the martial metaphor?
I don't want things like 'fireworks'
or 'starlight' either. The oil spill is better,
but then that's making sex with me
topical when it should be newsworthy.
I know, I've got it. How about:
fucking me is like licking stamps?
Sticky, time consuming and capable
of taking you to destinations exotic and
mundane. Yes, I like that very much.

Joystick Valhalla

The radio tells me drones are reapers,
scythe-shaped saucers shearing the sky,
propelled from Big Rock Candy Mountain
by slow-blinking fat young men,
untroubled by RSI or PornTube wrist,
frolicking in an orgiastic joystick Valhalla,

where screens shield them from what's spilt
on the soil, six thousand leagues away,
laxly playing their games with dusty blobs,
making confetti out of wedding favours,
and never challenging their vow:
the only safe space is empty space.

We are Premier League

We are Nando's skin on X-box wings
We are charitable visits, making dreams come true

We are role models and bandwagon drivers
We are baby Bentleys on private roads

We are gold tattoos on choking necks
We are orange spider mohicans on the backs of heads

We are dating on *TOWIE* and fit well jel
We are boys made good on our roasts

We are court appearances in Armani suits
We are playthings of offshore corporations

We are sponsored elite, and we are endorsed
We've parked the bus and we want more

We are the wages of underachievement
We are 17th place and we are class

Bantz

we think about
every four seconds
it

eat pine, apples
drink pineapple juice
because

LAD pack do
away with mixers
spirits

no wenches at
pre-drinks testosterone
polluted

#justsayingyeah
I am Bantersaurus
Rex

sex god secrets
at the club
yes

black belt banter
tactical chunder seems
legit

keep calm sit
on my face
#leaveit

sex maths embarrassed
if not slip
one

skank shag better
then wank of
shame

the question – how
wet does it?
need

to be? vajayjay
rip my banjo
spit

big mac brick
burn up back
breasticles

niagra falls turn
over manual release
niagra

how much banter
is there even
such

a thing as
too much fucking
banter?

THIS BANTZ IS FOR THE PURPOSE
OF HUMOUR AND SHOULD NOT
BE TAKEN SERIOUSLY

Rave equations

If 1990 was time for the guru,
where now is x, what time is love?

Bass how exponentially low can
you go if you're on a ragga tip?

How many little fluffy clouds fit in
the big fish little fish cardboard box?

What is the standard deviation of the
Pacific state when Belfast chimes orbital?

Charly says voodoo ray.
Assess that probability.

What is the percentage that altern-8s
when you pump up the volume?

As this factorial is not over yet,
will you let me be your fantasy?

On enthusiasm

I asked Google to name a year
in which nothing happened –
a shy 12 months that had
shrunk away from the time line.

Instead it told me all about
the apocalypse that didn't arrive
in 2012, and while I wanted to chide it
for confusing 'the end' with 'nothing',

I couldn't help but smile at the manner
in which it proffered this terminal inexactitude
the way I used to in class, hand
wriggling on urgent flagpole arm,

chancing that being wrong was better
than quenching glee. If only someone
had told me that enthusiasm is also drowned
by all the nothings that accumulate –

the failure barnacles that make
the soul a marine carapace,
indulgently leaking towards
the histories you can't outsail.

Making a cheese soufflé rise

David Ogilvy is swashbuckling opposite me,
wreathed in the blue smoke of his success.
His expression says, "Do not think that advertising

is not a job for you, that you are too proud to sell.
I burnt my hands in kitchens in Paris, France,
and sir I can tell you these acts of persuasion

you undertake are nothing compared to making
a cheese soufflé rise under the gaze of an elite
brigade you can never join. And once you are done

examining your navel remember that this is a noble calling,
alerting the world, waking it up, a poster campaign for life.
You are the messenger of a good thing,

whatever your Frankfurt School says, a thing called progress,
a worthy thing for any man who calls himself a man.
Now, then. Go. Rise. Work."

The anniversary issue

I am forglopned*, struggling to load,
pixelated while walking down Wardour Street.

Greying personalities with media hair
pass me, talking about intertextuality

and Paul Morley, while I pretend
to be Eustace Tilley, the way you do

with the anniversary issue.
The queues queuing to get pancakes

beseech me instead to contemplate
the fact that DFW would have been 50

today, and that he and I will never
write the Great American Novel,

so my green card will forever be
a redundant bookmark. If only

there was a dummies' guide to help me,
like the one I am currently following

to write this New York School poem.
I don't mention any of this to the ex

I meet, merely contenting myself
with the standard envy at the sunny

contentment. I am left to discover
I have missed the *LRB* with the best verse

ever in it. I settle, to await my move
to an emirate, knowing that residing there

is a metaphor involving a lemon, a butterfly,
a monocle and the rest of my life.

*overwhelmed with astonishment

Writ

If I was Henry VIII
I'd reform my state,
give up my horses and plate,
wrap you in a cloth of gold,
marry you five more times.

Or maybe the better ruler to be
would be Shah Jahan,
so you'd get a Taj Mahal.
But then you'd be dead –

and you're best not as
a star chamber or tourist tomb,
but unrolled parchment,
waiting for the laws
that will bind us.

All the laurels in the world, and you give me these?

I woke up this morning
thinking I'd won the Prix
de l'Arc de Triomphe.

This is where love and capitalism
has got me, having me on that
I can win a horse race in Paris,

when it's obvious
I'm only any good over
the jumps at Wolverhampton.

Sister of the sun

The clouds are Tom-and-Jerrying for you,
while you prepare to roister a new continent
from its slumbers, and become a sister of the sun.

The ideology of sand will revive you,
and whichever of the six Californias you choose –
bear, peak, canyon, valley, empire or scene –

be untrammelled by the telegraph lines,
the silicon chips. Old world cities will weep
a new ocean that you will not side with them nor

trench hard along their boulevards, for now.
But when your celestial sibling finally meets
the waves, it won't be a disaster for all of us.

Towards a singularity

Talking about the end of time,
the gap was filled by two physicists –
"it will never happen".
Bent out of shape by the words,
my whisky rapier had no response.
Her weapon was heartfelt logic.
Clutching a white handbag shield,
wearing a leopard print armour coat,
she arrived in the King's Arms
outside of our normal hours.
The appointment was 5pm.

The appointment was 5pm,
outside of our normal hours.
She arrived in the King's Arms
wearing a leopard print armour coat,
clutching a white handbag shield.
Her weapon was heartfelt logic;
my whisky rapier had no response,
bent out of the shape by the words
"it will never happen".
The gap was filled by two physicists,
talking about the end of time.

Ticker-tape

She is where she always is at this point, sitting
in the Reverend's speakeasy, wingtips ascending,
waiting for the minute hand to move. A second

rolls over, becomes a new hour. I hold the tattoo
on her wrist, an outline – all dog legs and squat thrusts,
an obese pigeon unable to take off. She gathers herself:

My ticker-tape, my bracelet, my gimlet,
my green belt handcuff, my tube line, my roundel,
my encapsulation, my malachite collar,

my friend, my lover, my ambition,
my unconquered lands, my Western front, my Eiger,
my undocumented interior, my multiple timezones,

my endless vistas, my temples of display,
my pilgrimage, my refuge, my starting point,
my ever-changing slang, my exclusive code,

my palimpsest, my outline of the me I will become,
my dark market, my light house, my civilization,
my abecedary, my participatory incantation,

my sizzle and steak, my law-giving colophon,
my badge, my totem, my charm of luck,
my disgrace, my downfall, my encampment,

my erstwhile empire, my pier of pleasure,
my denial of service, my white tower,
my hundred crows rising, my convenient alliances,

my enemy of purpose, my flag of convenience,
my restless wanderer, my pulsating imagination,
my time lord, my endless riot, my kin of kin,

my zipless fuck, my zone of disobedience,
my end of the line, my capsule of forgiveness,
my one more for the road, my why-ever-not,

my seized day, my clenched fist,
my tunnels of indifference, my fashion galore,
my daring wonderings, my candy floss, my sugar loss,

my gadget of invention, my caffeine kick, my traction,
my exit wound, my magnificent workshop,
my typeface of command, my minded gap,

my for all, my luxurious lap, my officer of truth,
my light power and speed, my descent to brightness,
my weaponized umbrella, my catchpenny seasons,

my bye-law contraventions, my stolen impressions,
my dynamic dynamite, my matchday rattle, my cup final,
my imperial trial, my undampened enthusiasm,

my peddler's cries, my hawker's dilemmas, my bright hours,
my super club, my neon trapeze, my maximum meaning,
my expeditionary force, my pursuit of glee,

my mercenary moods, my mendicant bears,
my subtle delights, my peacock smiles, my rainbow hosts,
my flash exquisites, my hatful of ideologies,

my jumble of engineering, my votive village, my dirtee fowl,
my whistle display, my beak club boys, my typing pool girls,
my meat back room hooks, my variety pack,

my linear portraits, my proud ornaments,
my statuary obfuscations, my way of business,
my moving spirits, my fair fairs, my well-baited hoopla,

my compelling invitation, my misplaced discretion,
my coat of years, my solid comfort, my quirky legend,
my wonderground, my Byronic charm, my Blakean spells,

my Wildean wilds, my Magnificent Ambersons, my herb of work,
my workaday history, my ego limerick, my double-sheet facts,
my mirror-real ticket, my manorial extension, my open system,

my Whitsuntide outing, my sunset sanctuary, my concrete lady,
my silver river, my surfeit resort, my closed conspiracy,
my colour trooping, my oyez sport, my monarchtopolis,

my mother's promises, my digital handshake,
my dictatorial signature, my distress bleeps,
my transparent telegrams, my constant change,

my ghosts of progress, my administrative burden,
my chains of buffonery, my griffin barriers, my dirty martini,
my impatient regret, my unbound determination,

my differential equations, my regression to the mean,
my standard deviation, my soda siphon, my power ballads,
my tongue thieves, my tied brewers, my spiced negroni,

my stereotypical cliché, my bomber command, my secular hymn,
my paradisal playground, my seducer's lair, my casino bank,
my pie and mash, my fizzing diamonds, my broadcast booth,

my 78rpm shellacking, my flotilla of pratfalls, my corporate bequest,
my boutique philosophy, my jubilee of consumption, my credit card debt,
my inevitable performance, my battalions of redoubt, my bases of plenty,

my fleet of suns, my bestiary of incompetence, my flood plain of
    irrelevance,
my balsam hopes, my dockside griefs, my Festival of Britain,
my cistern of rubrics, my incendiary rage, my *noblesse oblige*,

my revolutions, my *force majeure*, my manifesto of sorts,
my quack illnesses, my prescriptions of choice, my harlots of nonentity,
my endless parabola, my arc-ing rise and fall,

my one two three four five senses working o-ver-time,

my sniveling politeness, my shopping malls, my pimple's engagement,
my cybernetic jungle, my Westway curse, my recycled contentments,
my gas bottle bogeys, my party *pris* vegetables, my discreet seraglio,

my twittering bloodstream, my barbers of togetherness,
my aces of razors, my ruffians of now, my porcupines of pique,
my forced antiquities, my pose of purpose, my entrepreneurial gland,

my reverent mindset, my master of ceremonies, my wild goose chase,
my tame brute attack, my demonic infestation, my bubonic epicentre,
my hyperbolic hymnal, my ministering tides, my big society philippics,

my food bank requests, my sheltering minstrels, my homeless tirades,
my storm-force entanglements, my business card soldiering,
my fake platoons, my public affections, my transgressions of trivia,

my uncreative writing, my zooming symbology, my formalist desires,
my imponderable castles, my church of repute,
my distinct chairs, my national hero, my tallow fat candles,

my plucked stings, my cosmic vibrations, my cool reports,
my missing retorts, my noble ways to die, my top hat blues,
my cane permissions, my excellent thoughts,

my endless perorations, my shellshocked terminology, my Afrobeat,
my temple graces, my wigged-out masterclasses, my poaching pompadour,
my despicable grading, my 2009 vintage, my leap of sharps,

my generational imbibing, my rhetorical ecstasy,
my graduate imbalances, my impermanent incentives,
my grandiose lectures, my hotel for five to nines,

my gilded palaces of sin, my doomed charabancs,
my endless embodiments, my great stink, my electrified presences,
my *beau monde* travails, my suburban escarpment, my pressure drop,

my depth charge, my quip police, my ruler of measures,
my landscape of loss, my jaunty paradiddle, my askew gloom,
my parroted wisdom, my score of scores, my hairshirt supremacy,

my knavish indolence, my astrological impulses, my zealous fool,
my riff on openness, my twin-hilled chariot, my kernel of the universe,
my hull of stead, my flirtatious dilemma, my rhyming eminence,

my inventive shift-pattern, my avant-garde calamity, my spatial ugliness,
my regular fries, my academic destiny, my coiled non-sequitur,
my seductive trope, my show of muscle, my leap of despair,

my despair of faith, my faith in leaps, my aleph, my infinite heft,
my exurban crawl, my putative republic, my doge's indulgence,
my drover's fealty, my myth of the beholden,

my scrambled synopses, my draining talent, my sinking outliers,
my bell-curve histrionics, my transformed probabilities,
my self-help charter, my examined lives, my life manual,

my big idea – *all of our big ideas*; my empirical workings,
my imploding industry, my pet peeve, my loyal trumpet,
my normative decisions, my acting of rites, my shock therapy,

my abandoned forecasts, my gay diatribes, my golden thread of belief,
my impecunious injunctions, my momentary comfort,
my bushwhacked shelter, my self-preservation society,

my dream possibilities, my gaudy minima, my incubatory desires,
my static impossibility, my matrilineal hedging, my matrimonial pool,
my Eastern chutzpah and Western greed,

my Northern charm and Southern bloom,
my displaced redevelopment, my righteous paths,
my preservation jams, my oblique strategies,

my art school crucible, my oratorical observations,
my narrowing clips, my sclerotic placing, my juggernaut pacing,
my locked-in depravity, my buzz of the moment,

my viral irregularity, my vulgar alarms, my simplistic tantrums,
my custodian's embrace, my questionable resolve,
my tactical whispers, my robotic wherewithal,

my lupine howl, my bovine capitalism, my perturbed foxiness,
my stomping illegality, my ring of steel, my red route girdle,
my polyphonic milieu, my dragon strut, my unicorn twinkle,

my dead astrolabe, my telescopic prowess, my telepathic intimacy,
my reluctant demeanour, my pouting grip, my posturing defiance,
my duty of concern, my grasping memory, my amorous frivolity,

my thwarted orgasm, my building frustration,
my corseted detumescence, my suspended creation,
my sooty nostalgia, my smokestack glory,

my unleashed shawl, my boa constrictor,
my lost whale, my riverbank tales,
my practical fetters, my fake gallop, my coachman's sense,

my squandered sensibility, my plausible denial, my city sickness,
my gallery superlatives, my swindling bacteria, my celebrity stature,
my harrowing nature, my macaronic fulcrum, my masonic pendulum,

my cutpurse serenity, my perfect hat-trick, my smooth flow of ink,
my incidental detail, my biblical revelation, my brewing melody,
my fantastical trailer, my energetic thinker, my archival gobbet,

my ballroom feeler, my rape of the lock, my juvenile lockdown,
my imminent dispatching, my hard-cover bonding,
my rough guide to the future, my exclusion zone, my back alley seduction

my limping village, my forever hamlet, my lipstick payoff,
my pounding frugality, my sibling rivalry, my money shot,
my first edifices, my nobody complexes, my beautiful certainties,

my skidding dilemmas, my panoramic protest, my shoebox condiments,
my wheedling cognition, my content grasping, my glancing culture,
my nonsense chromatics, my edible dilemmas, my marginal comments,

my annotated resignation, my anointed one, my hipster table,
my single coincidence, my clunking breath, my vitriolic anthem,
my burning effigy, my independence declaration,

my miraculous unions, my startling tomb, my crowned emptiness,
my frozen divination, my comedic impudence, my naked obsession,
my vulnerable esophagus, my dismissed biology, my blurred imperative,

my aerobic fitness, my engineered obsequies, my unplanned obsolescence,
my chartered beliefs, my champagne fascism, my communitarian impulse,
my unexpected stance, my tricyclic sunrise, my dance-card diplomacy,

my beats per minute, my roulette degradation, my conscious presence,
my bloodied hands, my intrusive drowning, my deliberative scanning,
my audible grind, my climate-controlled shape, my gestural interface,

my timely snapshot, my ambassadorial prerogative, my devil may care,
my standard operating procedure, my endless prayer,
my gristle powder, my blood washing, my purring engine,

my alchemical set, my pungent university, my tapestry of attachment,
my innate condition, my human tradition, my unanticipated weakness,
my share-cropping existence, my harvesting dilemmas,

my grandmaster apologies, my godfathered regrets,
my impermanent staring, my *grand projets*,
my memorials of war, my fired bunting, my gadabout dancing,

my Piccadilly palare, my gerrymandered heart, my valve thinking,
my value singing, my comprehensive settlement, my private scepticism,
my Heath Robinson, my marvellous schtick, my charismatic stick,

my productive lifecycle, my Pareto efficiency, my surveilled windows,
my despised aorta, my penny farthing conundrums,
my white-feather fucks, my contemptible bargains,

my science of sweet, my non-exclusive licence, my zeitgeist strafing,
my willing accomplice, my pivotal distraction, my lying hoard,
my slice of toast, my half of life,

my sky-bottling days, my modest proposal, my tale of woe,
my inheritance tax, my eggshell brocade, my bathrub taser,
my rich vein of loam, my looming catastrophe, my strophe of idolect,

my covers band, my radio head, my Walbrook delta,
my sensory overload, my unpeeled entity, my planned penury,
my dark side taxi, my demand shock, my supply reforms,

my algorithmic certainty, my taxonomic exactitude,
my gameday focus, my cheerleader passion,
my terminal gallstone, my dying leaderene,

my blank-faced charivari, my heathen god, my pagan lover,
my uncertain bride, my waterlogged piano, my one-line thesis,
my symbol of optimism, my eureka moment,

my regret minimization framework, my choice architecture,
my mincing palette, my convivial conurbation,
my processional vogue, my wayward coxcomb,

my farewell century, my melting villain,
my cornfed prince, my milksop illusion,
my indigestible pangs, my phallic stamps,

my breast beating, my heartless seesaw, my pleated furrow,
my casual interaction, my intimate engagement,
my penal exactitude, my conscripted *billets-doux*,

my happy anomie, my endless parade,
my data-driven enclave, my glittering messages.
My city. My belonging. I am waiting to fill it in.

Redzone

The stadium clocks are sprinting down;
one second to go until the last time out
becomes permanent. I have been game-
managing with oblique slights and feints,
but now in the redzone I am fast revealed
to be a rookie, a specialist in small plays.
An eye flips up, a headset mic drops –
before the lashes I am to be coached:
The stars aren't yellow penalty flags to
avoid; don't be scared by this aperture
to explode into – *to love is to play is to risk
is to win*. I will scoop up your forced fumble
but I cannot wait if you want me only after
the fireworks of your current half-time show.

Cheerleader

She is driving a Mustang, of course;
top down, coloured 'Vermillionaire', of course.

Glowing into the booth, singeing my toes,
she orders a root beer and double chilli fries,

triple cooking them again before popping
them in, salting her eyebrows as she goes.

She is all *Vogue* shoot this, NASA guy that,
letting loose congressional secrets, the confessions

of worshippers. Dimming for a moment, she sinks
then blares: don't blame me I didn't love you

in high school. What's a cheerleader to do
when she has to get everyone up in the morning?

If I'd known all my suitors would be mathletes
not quarterbacks, I might have changed my mind.

Arguing with Mondrian about space

How right angles are not
    the right angles,

but clearly what we are
    actually arguing about is time,

and how, dynamically, I can push her
    to an equilibrium.

Ah, he says, that's the ol' double line
    rhythm conundrum –

she has you trapped in a plane
    of indecision.

Do not be blue about this,
    or gather the reds about you;

remake your internal atelier again,
    add more coloured panels,

especially her happy yellows.
    Make sure there is room for two.

Secrets need confidence and force

she said, as she snapped out
of her electric blue tights
and tied me to the bed.
But now it's five to seven
in our five to seven
and I'm feeling the strain:
I'm sure she'll leave me,
a second, decisive time.

The last neon sign maker in Hong Kong

His hands flutter by the five tongues of flame,
joints articulating at 800 degrees Celsius,
lips blowing commercial wishes down glass tubes,
speaking of honest scripts for certain characters:
light-heads, bending, swirling, inflating.

Thousand layer paper slides in to protect
the messages, before chicken intestines
shake hands with neon breath and iron hearts
for a brighter light: "without displays of prosperity
my city is a ghost town."

If you're feeling blue
the answer is argon, he says, but best
is daylight red. A door above an air con
unit glows rainbow ready, the past slipping out.
He inhales the urban gas one last time.

Code: pink and red and blue

I saw you today and thought wow,
have they issued an all ports warning
that you're on the loose, looking like that?

By 'that' I mean 'dangerous' of course,
not 'bad'; but yes, bad too,
in the sense of you making me

think things I probably shouldn't.
What can I say about you
(other than 'Oh, you're undecipherable!')

that won't get me into trouble?
Come and set up a hideout
with me under the duvet,

and I will tell you about a man
with an unlikely beard and intense eyes
who told me I had a lucky face,

and when I look at yours I sometimes
want to find him to shake his hand and say,
sir, you may just have been right.

Gunmetal

(for Ian E)

The sky vibrates like Mussolini's mistress's dentures
in a Waterford tumbler

The sky throbs precipitately pink like the ululating
oestrogen of a Take That fan

The sky is a "precious, precious green Edmund,
a precious, precious green"

The sky is as cold as an ersatz gazpacho made out of
a homeopathic Aldi tomato

The sky is as playfully obtuse as an obscure collection
of Flaming Lips B-sides

The sky is as rigorously gloomy as a Bank of England
economic prognostication

The sky is an edition of *Noel's House Party*: full of gunge,
and the sound of a booming God laughing at our pratfalls

The sky is a flying change of leg in the dressage

The sky is a Tao Lin Google Chat endlessly referring to its
own digital circularity

The sky is not the sky: it is the sea having got terribly
confused at JobcentrePlus

The sky is an engine powered by steam and onions and
polystyrene chips

The sky is just fucking awesome, ok, and doesn't need
a weapons-based simile to make it so

The valley of the infinite

His dream of here _ the park and the bay and the bridge _ had been animated by a simple koan that, to his shallow ears, promised a bright release.

'The valley of the infinite' _ it had never been made clear what this boundlessness was, or what it might be for. It sounded thrilling. West was where it was.

It left him breathless to be a pico-scale part of it. He revelled in knowing that he was seeingdoingmakingliving the products, the patterns, the progress the rest of the world would follow a second, a year, an aeon later. The BA, the MA, the MBA, the JD, the various stints of intrapreneurial interning with ramrod WASP elite firms, disguising their lack of proximity to the bleeding edge by sprinkling the suffix '.io' over their business cards; all had been worth it to bring him to the flaking lip of *now*.

Except that he had become too caught up in the *now* to recognise that he had slipped into the *then*. He found his skillset declared suboptimal, his personality fit deemed inexact, his passcard inoperative.

He tried one last processing, to interrogate where this thought, this mania _ this yearning desire _ for the promise of The Golden State had come from, and he could only surmise that it was his father's radio, tuned to a station that brought news of pitches and swings, bunts and no-hitters, from a somewhere called Candlestick Park. It sounded heart-breaking even then.

He swung _

Pretanic

(A journal of some proceedings on the
North Atlantic archipelago)

The British genius
#MyEngland
**What's the matter with [insert (non-metropolitan)
English constituency of choice]?**
Diagnosis: 'Londonism'
Strategies to save the Union
Tom Paine's submarine
The problem of becoming English

The British genius

isn't for financing things or inventing games,
teaching them to others, playing them fairly,
then badly and still turning up. No, it's actually me:
all the conversation, the hot air if you like,
that powers everything, anything of worth
(note, not of value) that we do. All those lawyers,
advertisers, politicos, pundits, journos,
stuttering aristos, dare I say it poets too;
what do you think they run on? The charm,
the listless seduction, where do you think they
come from? You know why the shipping forecast
is the nation's secular hymn? It's not for sailors;
it's for those in the navy of hyperbole, so they
know where to find me, to refill their sails.

#MyEngland

#MyEngland is Burberry headscarves in cockney accents.

#MyEngland is top hats drawn in chalk.

#MyEngland is Australian gym girls eating sticky buns.

#MyEngland is hi-viz jackets at rest.

#MyEngland is Teletubby hills in urban playgrounds.

#MyEngland is buccaneers, corner cutters and grit.

#MyEngland is capital and tides and enclosures and rollercoasters.

#MyEngland is dragons and poets duelling at closing time with
    miniature Spitfires.

#MyEngland is pavilions and wall games and skills sharpened on kerbs.

#MyEngland is a pageantry of theatrical boos at a corner kick.

#MyEngland is a set of Imperial calling cards with empirical effects.

#MyEngland is an 8-bit commonwealth, a yawning heptarchy.

#MyEngland is uxorious towards customs and those forgotten
    in churchyards.

#MyEngland is grave towards hypocrisy, except in its back gardens.

#MyEngland sees technology as a matter of string and disambiguation.

#MyEngland is reinventing the world, one market at a time.

#MyEngland is waiting for a new joint to arise.

#MyEngland is art rock poses in suburban situations.

#MyEngland is the scene that celebrates itself.

#MyEngland is a sound system playing Elgar, filtered through jerk chicken.

#MyEngland is pundits holding court in bungalows over imported
    convenience food.

#MyEngland is a demonstration around a campfire in a dell.

#MyEngland is minor shires competing for pewter tankards in
    administration.

#MyEngland is wise counsel, disguised as affairs on park benches.

#MyEngland is a university of hedgerows, the analogue, the divine.

#MyEngland is This Great Movement of Ours.

#MyEngland is the first nation, the future nation, the nation formerly
    known as.

#MyEngland is magic and rain, a flutter on the hope that roses might
    flutter for you.

What's the matter with [insert (non-metropolitan) English constituency of choice]?

(with apologies to Thomas Frank)

It's as if we still have whiplash
from that brainbreaking exit poll,
accurately pointing to the crash:
voteless dreams exacting a toll.
What now for a nation fissiparous?
No chance this lot'll be magnanimous.
The things we've in common they forget,
loosening the straps of the safety net.
But there is light when we look round,
(their brand is not detoxified,
hence why their supporters are shy)
if we leave the moral high ground.
Forget complain–

*Look I'll go back and finish the sonnet in a bit, but
seriously can you please stop calling people who voted to
the right of you* evil*? They're not – ill-informed maybe,
only looking as far as their front door or their street, but
they are not baby eaters. If you start in that register, how
can you ever hope they might listen to you when you try
and win them back? I have been on the left long enough to
know that a cry of betrayal is never far away, but it's really
not a good look to suggest that it was the voters wot did
the stabbing in the front. And don't take this to mean that
I am any less committed to social justice – I voted Labour,
I gave money to the campaign, hell I cried on election
night – but seriously, we can sit around bemoaning all the
forces arrayed against us, or we can work with the grain
of England to try and find this fabled progressive majority*

that still might be out there. I'll take ends over means most
days if we can save what we have before starting again.
Practically? Hell I don't know, but we have to get out
from behind our screens and in to the world. As it turns
out that's still where politics lives – who knew? And when
we're out there, let us try treating it as a carnival of joy
instead of a festival of I-Told-You-So-ism, served with a
side of slathering vitriol. Rationality isn't enough, harping
on about how our values are superior isn't enough – put
some fizz in your pieties! Fuck it, rebrand the Welfare State
as the Welfare Trampoline if you like, but Jesus we will
not win if we do not offer something that looks like a smile
wrapped around the weapons we'll need to fight the fear we
know is coming. Right, done. Kthnxbai.

–ing, we need to persuade;
the new Jerusalem has only been delayed.

May 2015

Diagnosis: 'Londonism'

(a/k/a Paging Dr Pangloss, you might need
to extend your rounds)

The panjandrum in his glass and steel lair
scans the wealth flowing across the river,
pulls up his chalkstripe pantaloons to declare:
you drones, we are not sick nor quivering.

The jobs are rich, filling and bountiful;
the inflation is flat and negligible,
the environment pleasingly perishable –
this economic model impregnable.

I know this because the bankers tell me so;
the politicians agree, then crow –
and my shoe leather is too precious
to walk beyond the green belt that chokes us.

I cannot help that I know more than you,
that my facts will always beat your facts,
because they come from gleaming technocrats,
the new look, new establishment crew.

Join me in celebrating this urban supremacy!
Embrace this rationalism so filigree!
What must we know of life beyond zone 6?
It is a fine rumour, but does not exist.

Strategies to save the Union

In front of invited starched bankers do an English emote,
warn of the wallet-threatening perils of any currency float.

Grumble and peeve about the future's lack of workable plan Bs,
draw charts of the forthcoming Cairngorms of redundancies.

Offer to watch *The White Heather Club* on an endless repeating jag,
make the Saltire bigger in a newly redesigned flag.

Ritualistically sacrifice one of the forgettable minor royals,
attack any traditional appeals to Pictish blood and soil.

Wheel out whoever's left of the low road's émigré elite,
to deploy celebrity love bombs and despairing #dontgo tweets.

Hit the hysteria max button on the crisis-making machine,
whisper about the welfare from which you'll have to be weaned.

Promise a real, *no really real*, devolution of power this time,
say with fingers crossed, *we two peoples – honest, we still rhyme.*

Tom Paine's submarine

At some point in the fatuous flotilla, I dream I see
a periscope pop up by King's Reach, and Thomas Paine
surface in a one-man submarine, having come back to
check on us and semaphore out this common sense hymn:
    Boys and girls, I gave you the playbook
    and you give me this? River traffic jams and
    sycophancy disguised as red, white and blue treacle?
    I wanted fanfares for all of you, not for one
    uncommon persistence, but I fear you have been
    seduced by the inertia, the dazzle and the bunting.
    Break those jubilee lines! Unpick her ermine corset!
    Burn the empire-tipped spears! And when you
    dance around the bonfire, tell yourselves:
    we are all the wearers of crowns.

The problem of becoming English

wasn't, as I was supposing,
of whether the ethnicity
would accept my race;
but rather one of posing
in a top hat for publicity.

Δ

Coming soon in edition 2 of **Pretanic**:

Tight Little Island
Impossible nation
Imperial cosmic sickness
History distortion field
The Overblown Age
Eating popcorn at the apocalypse
¯_(◎)_/¯

Point of departure

(for James Cameron)

Not for me chutzpah's champions or imposters' manifestoes.
Hucksters' hagiographies have me heaving.
I cannot read blaggers' ballads, the fables of fluent fabulists,
tales of derring 'you-did-whatters?' without a shudder,
a shiver, that embarrassment's fist will reach into
my digger-bucket jaw, pull out my lily heart
and say to the digitised nano audiences, *well,*
deep down you all knew. And now you *can stop*
wondering whether we will find you out this time.
The irony is, of course, that despite the blips of outrage it –
I – will be forgotten as fast as the sea forgets a wave.

A man is on the TV, telling me about

A man who is urbane, a realist, *a man who knows,* is on the TV, telling me about███████A man who cares about the white cuffs of his shirt remaining pristine is on the TV, telling me about███████████A man who dreams he was born under the skirts of a discarded Army greatcoat is on the TV, telling me about██████A man who slavishly chases proximity to power is on the TV, telling me about███A man who talks to securocrats in clubs and leaves his credulity in the cloakroom is on the TV, telling me about████████A man who knows the moral complexities and grey areas of the wine list is on the TV, telling me about ██████████A man who has done quite well out of the unthinking echo chamber of the Western military-industrial complex is on the TV, telling me about████████A man whose word processor is nicknamed 'Destroyer of Islamofascists' is on the TV, telling me about ██████A man who fired the starting pistol on the clash of civilisations is on the TV, telling me about████████████A man who thinks he is the new TE Lawrence is on the TV, telling me about ████████████████A man who is euphemistically happy is telling me about██████A man who thinks enhanced interrogation techniques work is on the TV, telling me about███████████A man who believes that efficacy trumps debate is on the TV, telling me about██████████ A man who chooses not to believe the testimony of a man who says, "I know from personal experience that the abuse of prisoners often produces bad intelligence because a person will say anything he thinks his captors wants to hear – true or false – if he believes it will relieve his suffering," is on the TV, telling me about ███████████A man who has forgotten that the awesome majesty of the oligopoly of violence tends to beat asymmetric attempts to thwart it is on the TV, telling me about ███ A man who has never been the other is on the TV, telling me about ███ A man who will never be mistaken for another man, taken, and then chained to a radiator and left to freeze to death is on the TV, telling me about ██████ A man who has never been redacted is on the TV, telling me about ███████ A man who has misplaced the knowledge that he is human is on the TV, telling me about

Risk patterns

1.

I'm hearing that foxes
are feeling put out
the chickens are gathering
in chicken-only meetings,
discussing how fox violence
makes them feel.

2.

We like the idea of the South.
Until it knocks on our door.

3.

Who is surprised that people
want to claim the joys of being 'exotic'
but none of the pain of being 'different'?

4.

The thing that really pulled me up:
half the country has fled. 50%, gone,
in less than two years.

Did *all* of them choose to do that?
Is it actually a choice when someone
shoves a gun in your face and says 'go'?

5.

(To the tune of 'Spider-Man')

Whiter-Man! Whiter Man!
Does whatever a hegemonic culture
lets him get away with, frankly.

6.

All those brown people
quietly condoning terrorism.

So unlike all those white people,
loudly condemning racism.

Oh.

7.

You know we're an island, right?
How do you think most people
got here first? They didn't fall
from the trees, or spring up fully formed
from the heather. Some sort of sea crossing
may have been involved.

8.

There'll never be much compassion in this debate.
How can there be when we've – *'we'! Look how I accept
it!* – done a lot of invading, and rarely been invaded?
Deep down, what we're expressing is the exasperation
that *those chaps over there* couldn't make a better go of
defending themselves against their others – unlike us.

9.

I have recurring dream,
in which I stand on the table
at the dinner party I'm attending,
say "I'm an immigration jihadist.
Let them all in. Let's start the
Throw Open All The Doors Party."
I wake up, and silently chide myself
for being braver asleep than awake.

10.

I am an expat.
You are a refugee.
They are a migrant.

11.

Naming the programme *Mare Nostrum*.
The fucking cheek. It's their sea too.

12.

You know the continent
is ageing rapidly? Dying in fact.
Who do you think is going to come
and look after your parents, seeing
as you don't do extended families?
And this is the welcome you give
to the people who will be keeping
your show on the road.

13.

Refuge is not just a place.
It's a state of mind.
A state of hope.

14.

I've already won the lottery.
I have a British passport.

Diversity campaign

This is a communication announcing the company's latest 'diversity' campaign.

First you see a happy-clappy message that says something piously right-on about how we strive to be different, in the way our customers are different. You know, Kumbaya Commercialism.

Following that here is a picture of four or five employees representing the 'rainbow of happiness' we'd like you to believe we are – the smiling, camp White man; the pretty, submissive East Asian woman; the Afro-Caribbean guy who we still feel is threatening so we've put him at the back; the South Asian wearing glasses – obviously he's good with numbers. Although we never manage to include the wheelchair user we're always meaning to.

(And don't get us started about educational achievement, class, nationality. We haven't been able to get started on this either, a state of affairs the chaps on the board have deemed 'regrettable'.)

Following the image is a spurious, and spurious-sounding target – *"We'll have a black transgender working class CFO by 2020!"* – which to untrained ears is *plausibly* achievable, if all you are doing is tutting when breezing through the comments below the article that really is the sole motivation as to why we're putting this out there.

This then leads into the peroration that our young grad – 23, loves *The Man Who Would Be King* – is very proud of, around *how* true *'diversity' is about embracing all our differences – maybe even thinking something uncomfortable now and again –* but because he hasn't done a lick of Marxist history, doesn't actually follow this up to begin to worry about who has power and where it lies, or indeed this current mode of capitalism, a model that fails to acknowledge that it might not inherently work without y'know, the operating defaults and remnants of slavery and / or imperialism.

And underneath, finally, the postscript that you'll barely notice: that real success looks like never having to run a 'diversity' campaign ever again.

Here ends the communication. Frankly, we're done with ticking the box.

The campaign for mapping generic terms for streams in the contiguous United States

Brevetted for gallantry? Ready to take up your
commissions? Then the battle of the wilderness
is about to begin!

The instant we contact we are turned
into statues, all over the map. We lead each
other, find our ruins, borrow the light

and not worry about repayment. We are
alone, or something like it, draining our psychic
wealth, because we know it is that, not rain

that will drench us. We chant Ecclesiastes,
count the punctuation, read the Russians,
because we know there is something new

under this sun. We row on ceaselessly,
until we get stuck in the mud, with squibs
in our mouths, fireworks in theirs –

we are awed by the quiet eruptions. In
letters back and forth we remind our
sweethearts what we are in search of:

bright colour toponyms. Our sugar pumps
ask *what are they?* – we say, our honeymoon
highways, our new languages, our old rhetorics:

our *runs* our *forks*, our New Netherland *kills*,
our *swamps* and *sloughs*, washed out *washes*,
lime green *bayous*, *rios*, *arroyos* and *cañadas*

(not Canadas, that's another campaign entirely)
others have conquered before us. And what of
our branches and brooks, don't they get a look?

Well yes, a Dixie glance, as the alligator army
climbs out of its stream, ready to board the
relevant railroad, that follows the rivulet,

the same way foxes dress as lions, in the hope
of putting wolves to flight. Someday this campaign
too will end, and we will lament all the sunsets

we won't see in these places, even though it
sinks the same everywhere; we shall be
left with some autographs, the sentiment that

the home-sickness is a nostalgia, and the
memories of the last good time that this
country ever had.

Methuselah and the Link-Girl

The fear is, of course, that this is
how we will end up: tears running
into my Tolstoy beard, lamentations
that the painter and decorator
didn't get my *Dorian* right,

while you – and the sneer that snared
me, the wit that speared me,
the kohl that subdued me – go
on and on and thrillingly on.

You keep tweeting about your plans
to dye your mane again a murky
shade of attention; and I can't tell you
my one wish: just to hold your
new hair back from your face.

These things boys do

I am an eel passing far out, a slitherer in the seminar. I do
not volunteer that I was once accused of stalking a *dulcinea* –

– I didn't know how to put my rotting catch of love in a net,
drag it to sell to the implacable in Tsukiji fish market, Tokyo.

Hina reminds me shedding clothes is not the same as shredding
Englishness. But we might all have to be trial lawyers in bed;

capital wants us, wants us to be fluidly equable, but desire
only comes from friction: a touch, an impression, a catching –

the necessary luxuries. No one mentions the angels in muscles,
the joy of dopamine, being tied up with scarves that have

'attention' knitted into them. We need to get out of ourselves,
kidnap the brain, duct tape it still. Do you remember the ticker-

tape of pleasure that parades through you when you're touched
just right? *The body is good business* announces my she-god.

What night is

Hearing Big Ben from the window, not Radio 4.
The scamper of new paws across floorboards.
The knowing whine of the Kennington Fox.
You, breathing, whispering, turning.

Theseus' ship

(a triolet for Keisha Buchanan)

The last first babe left today,
on board Theseus' ship.
She's sailing far, far away.
The last first babe left today.
A new sugagirl has joined the fray;
let's hope she enjoys the trip.
The last first babe left today,
on board Theseus' ship.

Notes

'The summers of Camus' youth' is a based on an ... quote you can find here: http://www.laphamsq... Camus lines-work/mother-possibility ...ly.org/

Notes

'The summers of Camus' youth' is a based on an Albert Camus quote you can find here: http://www.laphamsquarterly.org/lines-work/mother-possibility

The title 'THE PACIFIC OCEN IS BECOMING CAFFEINATED' was stolen from: http://grist.org/pollution/the-pacific-ocean-is-becoming-caffeinated/

'Matchstick Empire' was inspired by an anecdote in, and borrows a phrase from, *The Three Emperors* by Miranda Carter.

'Arguing with Mondrian about space' was a runner up in the 2014 Troubadour International Poetry Prize, under a different title.

'The last neon sign maker in Hong Kong' arrived after watching: https://www.youtube.com/watch?v=EsIo57pH-pA

'Point of Departure' is for James Cameron (1911–85), a British journalist famous in his day as a foreign correspondent; he was also a founding member of the Campaign for Nuclear Disarmament. You can read about him, and the quote that lead to the poem, here: https://www.theguardian.com/theobserver/2003/dec/14/features.review157

'The campaign for mapping generic terms for streams in the contiguous United States' is a collision between Richard Brautigan's *Trout Fishing in America* and this map: https://flowingdata.com/2011/08/26/generic-terms-for-streams-mapped/

'These things boys do' was inspired by a seminar on desire hosted by Katherine Angel at Somerset House in January 2015. Thanks to Katherine for the invitation.

Acknowledgements

Some of the poems have been published in different guises in different places including: *And Other Poems, The Brautigan Book Club, Days of Roses, The Delinquent, here/there, LossLit, New Boots and Pantisocracies* (Smokestack Books), *Nothing In The Rule Book, Proletarian Poetry, Ten: The New Wave* (Bloodaxe), *Under the Radar, Verbatim Poetry, Visual Verse* and *Writers for Calais Refugees.*

With thanks to: Clare Pollard; Katy Evans-Bush; Jo Shapcott, Daljit Nagra and all at Faber Academy; Pascale Petit; Jill Abram and the Malika's Kitchen posse; my Complete Works family, especially Mona Arshi, Kayo Chingonyi and Nathalie Teitler for relentless boosterism; Mimi Khalvati and the seminar gang; and Jane Commane for much tea and wisdom.

Pictures: Ria Dastidar created the wondrous cover image, Naomi Woddis worked miracles with my portrait.

And my correspondents & cheerleaders: Holly Brockwell, Mark Cripps, Jo Cornish, Beth Emmens, Matt and Sheila Piper, Jonathan Thompson, Helena Watson; and Marie Hrynczak.

Not forgetting you dear reader: thank you for your coin and your time.

This book was mostly put together while listening to 'Gone Without Feeling' by The Black Ryder. For an optimum poetic experience please play this song at some point before, during or after reading.

Kthnxbai.